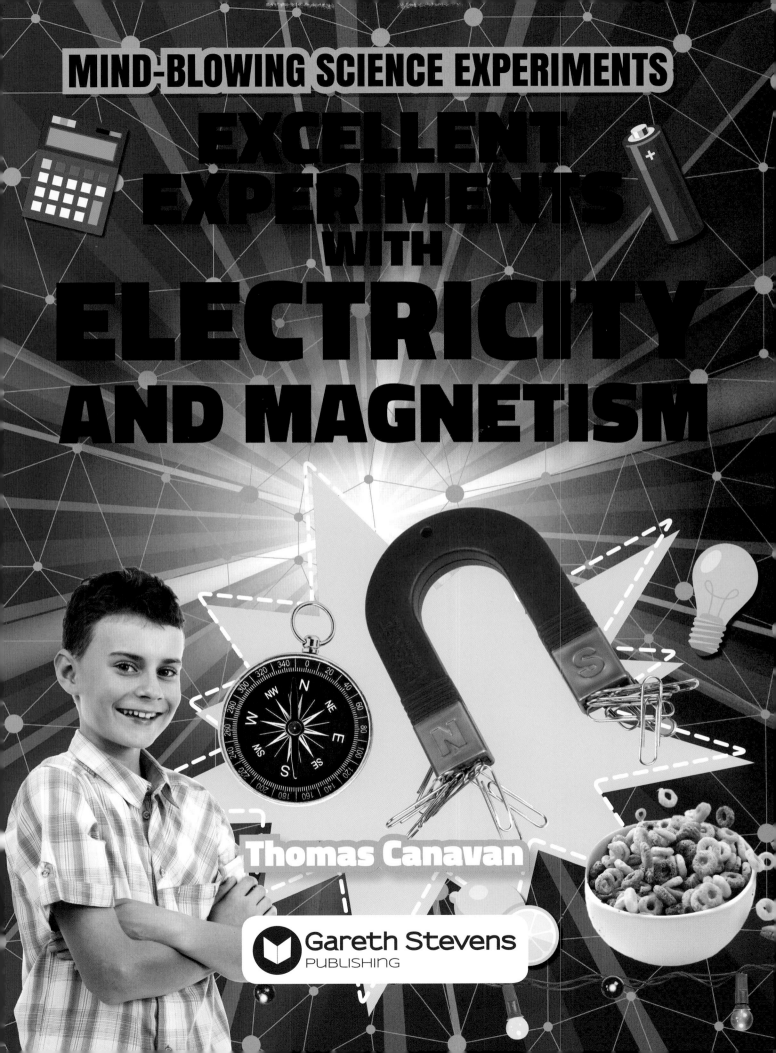

MIND-BLOWING SCIENCE EXPERIMENTS

EXCELLENT EXPERIMENTS WITH

ELECTRICITY

AND MAGNETISM

Thomas Canavan

Gareth Stevens
PUBLISHING

Please visit our website, www.garethstevens.com.
For a free color catalog of all our high-quality books,
call toll free 1-800-542-2595 or fax 1-877-542-2596.

Cataloging-in-Publication Data

Names: Canavan, Thomas.
Title: Excellent experiments with electricity and magnetism / Thomas Canavan.
Description: New York : Gareth Stevens Publishing, 2018. | Series: Mind-blowing science experiments | Includes index.
Identifiers: ISBN 9781538207505 (pbk.) | ISBN 9781538207420 (library bound) | ISBN 9781538207307 (6 pack)
Subjects: LCSH: Electricity--Experiments--Juvenile literature. | Magnetism--Experiments--Juvenile literature.
Classification: LCC QC533.C317 2018 | DDC 537'.078--dc23

Published in 2018 by
Gareth Stevens Publishing
111 East 14th Street, Suite 349
New York, NY 10003

Copyright © 2018 Arcturus Holdings Limited

Author: Thomas Canavan
Illustrator: Adam Linley
Experiments Coordinator: Anna Middleton
Designer: Elaine Wilkinson
Designer series edition: Emma Randall
Editors: Joe Harris, Rebecca Clunes, Frances Evans

All images courtesy of Shutterstock, apart from: Getty /
Digital Light Source: p. 33 t.

Printed in China

CPSIA compliance information: Batch CS17GS: For further information contact
Gareth Stevens, New York, New York at 1-800-542-2595.

Having Fun and Being Safe

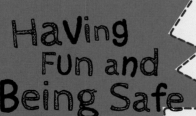

Inside this book you'll find a whole range of exciting science experiments that can be performed safely at home. Nearly all the equipment you need will be found around your own house. Anything that you don't have at home should be available at a local store.

We have given some recommendations alongside the instructions to let you know when adult help might be needed. However, the degree of adult supervision will vary, depending on the age of the reader and the experiment. We would recommend close adult supervision for any experiment involving cooking equipment, sharp implements, electrical equipment, or batteries.

The author and publisher cannot take responsibility for any injury, damage, or mess that might occur as a result of attempting the experiments in this book. Always tell an adult before you perform any experiments, and follow the instructions carefully.

Contents

A note about measurements

Measurements are given in U.S. form with metric in parentheses. The metric conversion is rounded to make it easier to measure.

Become an even brighter spark than you already are as you master the hidden power of electricity and magnetism!

Be a Tinsel Pilot

Jet engines, giant **propellers**, rocket fuel—these are some of the familiar methods for achieving flight. But electricity? Something sounds funny about an electric plane—unless it's the aircraft fuel of the future!

1

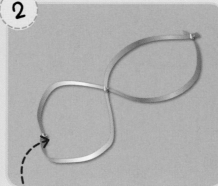

Tie the pieces of tinsel together about halfway along each length.

2

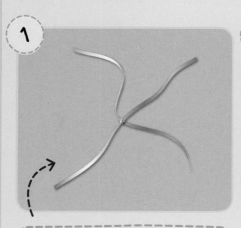

Loosely tie the four ends of tinsel in two pairs. This will form an "8" shape. Blow up the balloon and tie it shut.

3

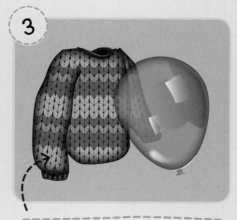

Rub the balloon vigorously against the sweater or scarf for about 15 seconds. Then hold the balloon in front of you. The side you rubbed against the wool should be facing up.

4

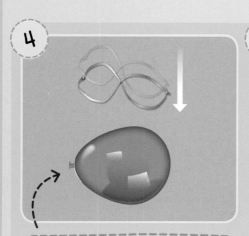

With your other hand, hold the tinsel above the balloon and let it drop.

5

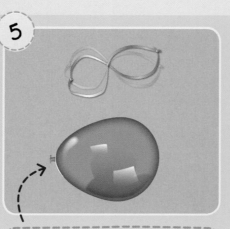

The tinsel should fall towards the balloon, then rise up again.

6

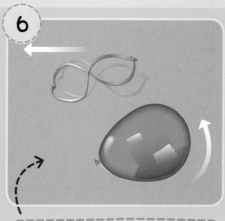

Keeping the tinsel hovering above the balloon, guide it through the air like a pilot.

HOW DOES IT WORK?

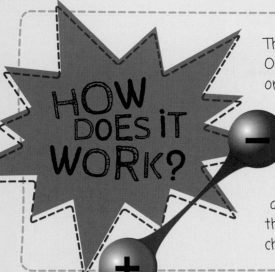

This experiment is all about attraction and repulsion. Objects with opposite electromagnetic charges attract, or pull towards, each other, while objects with the same electromagnetic charge repel, or push away from, each other. Rubbing the balloon against wool deposits lots of negatively charged **electrons** on the balloon's surface. Meanwhile, the tinsel starts off with a slightly positive charge. When you first drop the tinsel, it's attracted to the balloon. Then lots of electrons jump from the balloon to the tinsel. Soon, they both have a negative charge and repel each other.

TOP TIP!

If your tinsel doesn't rise, it might contain plastic that cannot be electrically charged. If this happens, just use a single piece of tinsel about 2–3 inches (5–8 cm) long.

WHAT HAPPENS IF...?

The **force** that's giving the tinsel its lift is electromagnetism, which has to do with positive and negative charges. But at what point will that force lose out to another force—**gravity**? You can test this battle of forces by repeating the experiment with three pieces of tinsel, then four, and so on. How many do you think you can launch before gravity wins?

REAL-LIFE SCIENCE

Loudspeakers use a combination of a permanent magnet and an electromagnet known as a coil. The permanent magnet sits inside a cone with the coil just in front of it. Electrical signals passing through the coil cause its magnetic field to shift back and forth, so that it's attracted to—then repelled by—the permanent magnet. All of this creates vibrations in the cone, and these vibrations create the sound waves that we hear as sounds!

The Electric Pencil

YOU WILL NEED

- A television
- A pencil
- A few friends to amaze

Some people refer to the television as a "flickering screen." If you want to know why, just try this simple experiment! You'll get an instant result, but the explanation takes a little longer to understand. Your audience might be happy to simply think of it as magic!

1

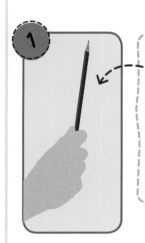

Ask some friends to sit facing a television. Hold up your pencil like a wand.

2

With the television off, quickly wave the pencil from side to side in front of the screen. Your friends should just see a blur.

3

Now turn the television on and repeat step 2.

4

Your friends should see several motionless pencils "stuck" in the path where you've waved.

HOW DOES IT WORK?

Televisions translate electrical signals into forms that we can understand with our senses—sounds and images. What we see as one moving image is actually a rapid series of still images. Electronic equipment scans the screen about 50 times a second. In this experiment, your hand waves the pencil quickly in front of the screen. At times, the pencil is moving in sync with the flashing, so that the image from a single flash (with the pencil in front of that still image) lingers in your mind.

TOP TIP!

You'll get the best effects if your movement is smooth (even if it's fast), rather than jerky.

WHAT HAPPENS IF...?

Now you know that the television's flashing lights are sending you a series of still images. To "stop" a moving object, you need to time its movement with the rhythm of the flashes. Ask an adult to place a fan in front of the television and then run the fan at different speeds. If its blades are rotating at a multiple of the flash (exactly 40 or 50 times faster) then you might see the blades "stop"! Why do you think that happens?

REAL-LIFE SCIENCE

The trick of "stopping" moving objects with quickly flashing lights is called the stroboscopic effect. It can be used in photography or filmmaking so that we can see fast movements more clearly, like a tennis ball hitting a racket or a raindrop splashing into a puddle. Engineers use this effect to check on quickly moving machinery while it is operating.

Funny Headlight

Don't be modest—you're pretty bright, aren't you? But are you bright enough to turn on a light bulb with just the hair on your head, a balloon, and no electrical equipment? Follow these steps to find out—the answer might surprise you!

1

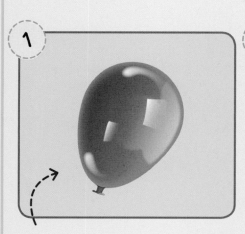

Blow up the balloon and tie it securely.

2

Rub the balloon back and forth quickly against your hair for about 30 seconds.

3

Hold the bulb vertically, with the two metal prongs facing up. Turn out the lights.

4

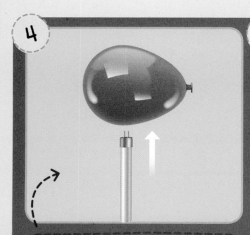

Place the side of the balloon you rubbed on your hair against the prongs.

5

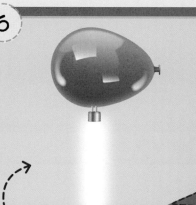

The light should glow noticeably while the balloon is touching the prongs!

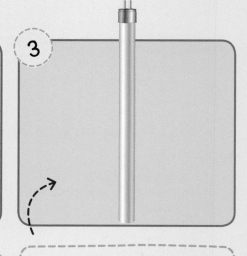

Be very careful with the bulb so it doesn't fall and shatter. You may need an adult's help!

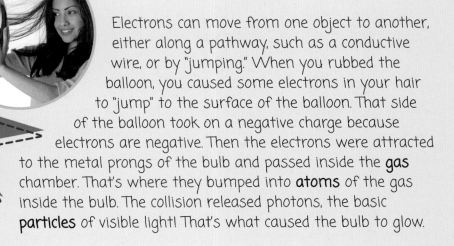

HOW DOES IT WORK?

Electrons can move from one object to another, either along a pathway, such as a conductive wire, or by "jumping." When you rubbed the balloon, you caused some electrons in your hair to "jump" to the surface of the balloon. That side of the balloon took on a negative charge because electrons are negative. Then the electrons were attracted to the metal prongs of the bulb and passed inside the **gas** chamber. That's where they bumped into **atoms** of the gas inside the bulb. The collision released photons, the basic **particles** of visible light! That's what caused the bulb to glow.

TOP TIP!

If you don't have a spare fluorescent bulb, you could ask an adult to remove one from a lamp for this experiment.

REAL-LIFE SCIENCE

You saw how a small amount of balloon-and-hair power could light your fluorescent bulb, so you won't be surprised to learn that these low-energy bulbs are extremely popular forms of **artificial** lighting. Older kinds of bulbs had to heat a wire until it glowed, which used far more energy than powering a fluorescent bulb.

WHAT HAPPENS IF...?

Imagine if you had the patience to rub the balloon against your hair for two or even three minutes. Would the balloon build up a stronger charge and make the light shine more brightly? Try to **predict** what would happen, then test your **hypothesis**!

The Bitter Battery

It's a hot summer night and you've just lost power in a thunderstorm. There's only one thing to do—open the freezer, find the ice cube tray, grab some supplies, and use it all to light the room! Well, maybe not the whole room—but you will be able to shed some light! Just follow the steps below.

YOU WILL NEED

- Plastic ice cube tray
- 5 tablespoons (80 ml) of vinegar
- 5 uncoated nails about 2 inches (5 cm) long
- An LED with two lengths of wire
- 19½ inches (50 cm) of copper wire
- Strong scissors or wire cutters
- Ruler

1
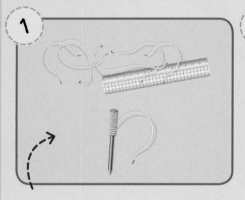

Cut the wire into five pieces, each 4 inches (10 cm) long. Wrap a wire around a nail, leaving about 2 inches (5 cm) unwound and sticking out.

2

Repeat step 1 with the other wires and nails.

3
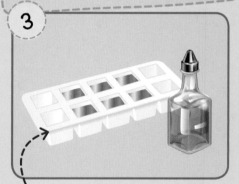

Fill six compartments (two rows of three) of the ice-cube tray with vinegar.

4
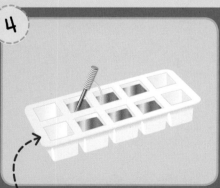

Place one of the nails in a corner compartment of the tray, with its length of wire placed in the next compartment.

5
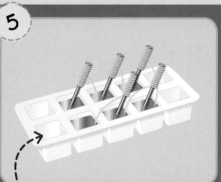

Repeat step 4 with all the nails. At the end you'll have the first compartment with only a nail and the last with only a wire.

6
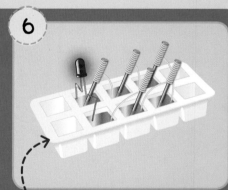

Carefully place one of the LED wires in the first compartment and the other wire in the last—the LED should light!

HOW DOES IT WORK?

You've probably noticed that the pattern of nails and wires finishes up where it started. This is called an electrical **circuit**, and it's the type of circuit used in **batteries**. Household batteries place two different types of metal within a type of **acid**. You've added two types of metal (wire and nails) to an acidic solution (the vinegar). The flow, or current, of electrons in the circuit passes from a wire through the vinegar to a nail, then through the wire and vinegar to another nail, and so on. That current is powerful enough to light the LED!

TOP TIP!

Make sure that none of the nails touch the loose wire ends.

WHAT HAPPENS IF...?

Vinegar is a good **conductor** of electrons, which is why it's perfect for an electric circuit. Try making a circuit using other household liquids such as lemon juice, water, or water with some salt sprinkled in. Which liquids work and which fail? Can you figure out why?

REAL-LIFE SCIENCE

Batteries power so many things we come across in daily life, from cell phones to laptops to electric cars. Engineers are constantly developing batteries that will hold longer charges or store larger amounts of electricity derived from solar energy.

Potato Power

If you were planning to explore a deep, dark cave, the last thing you'd expect to pack would be potatoes and nails. But maybe you'd think twice if you knew what they had in store. They just might light your way in a pinch!

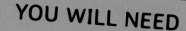
1

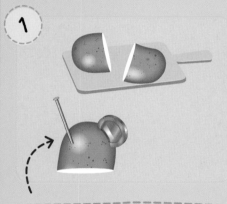

Cut the potato in half and lay the two pieces, flat side down, on a table or cutting board. Press a nail and a coin into one potato half, making sure they don't touch.

2

Attach one end of an alligator clip to the nail and one end of another clip to the coin.

3

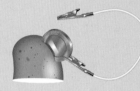

Press the second coin into the other potato half. Attach one end of the third alligator clip onto this coin.

4

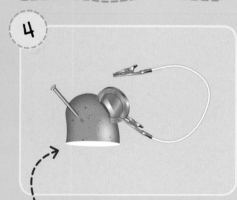

Add a nail to the second potato. Make sure it doesn't touch the coin.

5

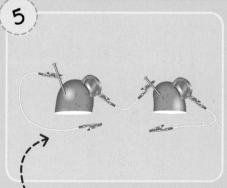

Attach the free end of the alligator clip connected to the first potato's coin to the second potato's nail.

6

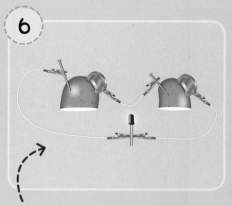

You should now have two unused clips. Attach each of these to one of the leads of the LED to light it up!

HOW DOES IT WORK?

The potato contains a mild acid, which eats away at the zinc coating of the nails and releases negatively charged electrons. That makes the nails the negative terminal of the battery. The same acid reacts with the copper in the coins, absorbing electrons in the process. Losing electrons turns the coins into positive battery terminals. With one metal (copper) losing electrons and the other metal (zinc) gaining them, the balance is upset. Electrons flow from one metal to the other to balance things out. This flow becomes the electrical current, which also runs through the LED, causing it to light up.

TOP TIP!

If the LED doesn't light up, attach the clips to the opposite wires. It's like putting a battery in the wrong way!

REAL-LIFE SCIENCE

This experiment calls for galvanized nails. Galvanizing is an industrial process that coats iron or steel with a layer of zinc. Your experiment worked because the acid in the potato chemically reacted with the zinc to release electrons.

Galvanizing is also a way of preventing another kind of chemical reaction. It provides a protective layer so that the iron or steel can't react with oxygen in the air. This stops the metals from rusting!

WHAT HAPPENS IF...?

Other vegetables and fruits contain an acid that can help produce a battery. You could use lemons, apples, and tomatoes. See which of these works best and compare them to your potato results. Turn the lights off just before you connect to the LED so you can compare results.

On a Roll

YOU WILL NEED

- Empty can
- Balloon
- Your hair or a wool sweater
- Table or smooth floor

You can understand some scientific principles more easily if you try them out in real life. The science might be complicated, but seeing it in action can be fascinating. Need help understanding electrons? Grab an empty can from the recycling bin and try this experiment!

1

Lay the can on its side on a flat surface such as a smooth floor or a large table.

2

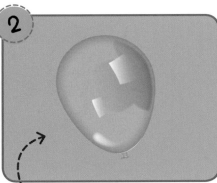

Blow up the balloon and tie it.

3

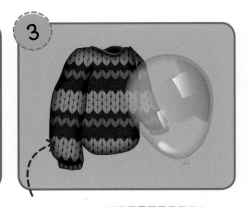

Rub the balloon vigorously against your hair or a sweater for 15–20 seconds.

4

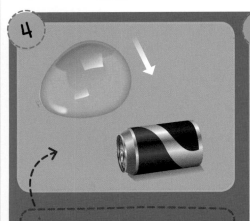

Lower the balloon towards the can. Be careful not to let them touch.

5

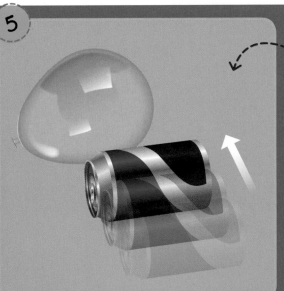

The can will start to roll towards the balloon. Get some practice attracting the can. You can even try to "lead" it across the surface by slowly moving the balloon.

HOW DOES IT WORK?

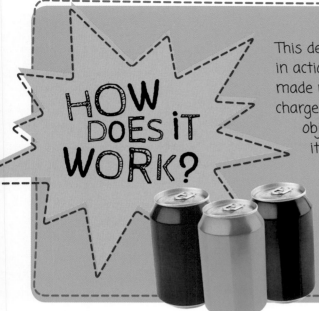

This demonstration is an example of **static electricity** in action. All matter, from a slice of pizza to a person, is made up of tiny charged particles. Electrons, the negatively charged particles, can sometimes be drawn from one object to another. That's called static electricity—and it's what you created when you rubbed the balloon against your hair! The balloon picks up electrons, and therefore a negative charge. That negative charge repelled some of the can's electrons. When they escaped, the can gained a slight positive charge, which attracted the can to the balloon.

TOP TIP!

You don't want to battle another force — **friction**. Make sure the surface is smooth and avoid carpets!

WHAT HAPPENS IF...?

You can change the course of moving water with static electricity! Rub the balloon on your head to charge it with electrons and then move it slowly towards a slow but steady flow of water from a tap. You'll see the stream of water move towards the balloon.

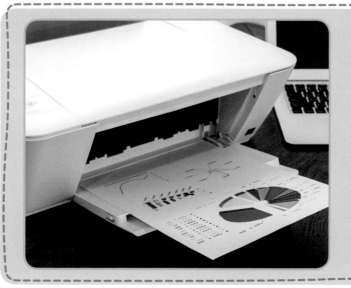

REAL-LIFE SCIENCE

Static electricity is all around you. Your computer screen's slight electrical charge attracts dust to it. You might feel a shock when you touch something metal after walking across a carpet—static electricity again. But scientists and engineers can also use static forces productively, from catching particles in exhaust pipes to guiding ink to the paper with laser printers.

Magnetic Breakfast

Lots of breakfast cereals advertise healthy ingredients such as vitamins. Some even claim to have iron! But do they really contain iron—as in nails and hammers? Is there any way of telling? Well, there's one way you might want to try.

YOU WILL NEED

- Breakfast cereal—make sure that it says "fortified" or "contains iron" on the box
- Cereal bowl
- Food processor
- Hot water
- Measuring jug
- Strong bar magnet
- Large ziplock freezer bag
- Chopping board

1

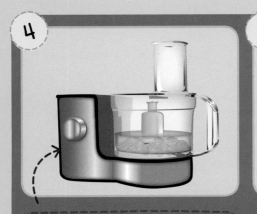

Pour an average portion of cereal into the bowl.

2

Transfer the cereal into a food processor.

3

Fill a measuring cup with 1 cup (250 ml) of hot water.

4

Pour that water into the food processor.

5

Run the processor for 30 seconds.

6

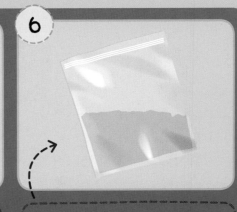

Pour the cereal mush from the processor into the freezer bag.

7

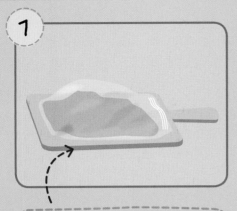

Carefully place the bag on the chopping board and slowly tip it down, making sure none of it spills.

8

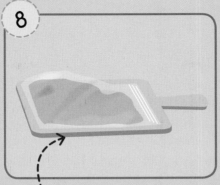

When it's on its side, with the air pushed out, seal the bag. It should be lying flat on the chopping board.

9

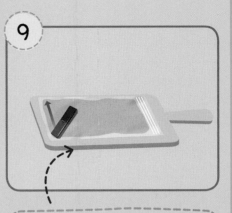

Press the magnet down on one corner of the bag and slowly push it across to the other side. Keep the same pressure on it the whole time.

10

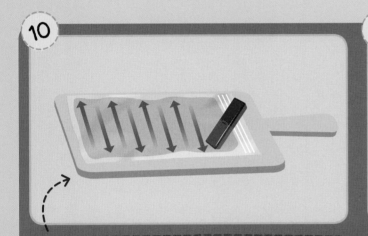

Keeping the magnet pressed down, work your way back and forth all the way to the other end of the bag — it should take a few minutes.

11

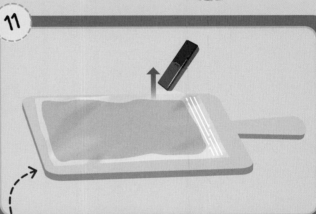

As you near the end of the bag, lift the magnet slightly. Some of the bag will probably stick to the magnet because of specks of iron being drawn to the magnet through the plastic!

TOP TIPS!

A white or lightly colored chopping board works best for this experiment.

If you don't have a food processor, you can pour the cereal-and-water mixture into the bag, seal it, and squeeze until it's mushy.

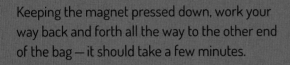

Continued

HOW DOES IT WORK?

Cereal manufacturers can't just put chunks of iron into your breakfast. You'd probably choke! Plus, you wouldn't care for the taste. This means that the iron must be in the form of tiny specks. Normally these would be invisible, but mashing up the cereal made it easier to separate the iron from the grains in the cereal. Just as a magnet can attract a chain of paper clips, your magnet picked up tiny specks of iron as you pressed it across the bag. By the end, you might have seen a ball the size of a pinhead made of iron bits!

WHAT HAPPENS IF...?

You should have seen some results from this experiment—flecks of iron extracted from the cereal mush with your magnet! You could try the experiment different ways. Would the water's temperature make a difference? What would happen if you didn't add any water? Do you think that you'd find more or less iron that way? Make some predictions and test the results.

REAL-LIFE SCIENCE

Iron is one of the most important nutrients that help our bodies work their best. It helps to draw energy from other nutrients and to keep red blood cells healthy and able to transport oxygen. We take in iron from the food we eat. Some foods—like your cereal—have added iron in case you're not getting it from natural sources, such as liver and leafy vegetables.

Homemade Compass

Have you heard of the Earth's magnetic north pole? Did you know that long magnets have ends called poles? Hmm...is there a connection there? Here's a chance to find out! You'll also learn how to navigate without a GPS, radio, radar, or even a map!

1

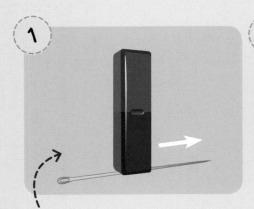

Hold the needle with one hand and stroke it five times in the same direction with the same magnetic pole.

2

½ inch

Ask an adult to slice the cork stopper to make a disc that is ½ inch (1 cm) thick.

Be careful using sharp knives, scissors, and needles. Ask an adult for help.

3

Push the needle carefully through the exact center of the cork disc.

4

Cut a circle from the card stock. Its diameter should be just shorter than the length of the needle.

5

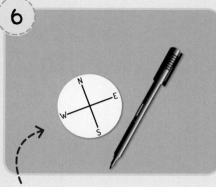

Use the ruler to trace two lines at right angles across this circle.

6

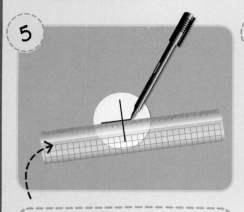

Mark the end of one line "N" for north and the opposite end "S" for south. Mark the end on the right "E" for east and the end on the left "W" for west.

7

Fill the sink with water and carefully place the cork disc on the surface.

8

One end of the needle will be pointing north. See "Top Tips!" to figure out which way is north!

9

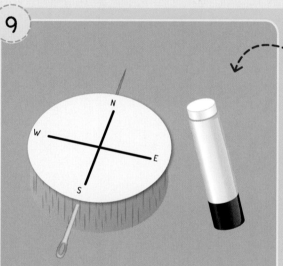

Glue the card stock disc to the top of the stopper so that the "N" lines up with the north pole of the needle.

TOP TiPS!

In step 1, lift the magnet away from the needle after each rub, then lower it again to the end where you began for the next rub.

If you're not sure which way your house faces, remember that the sun rises in the east, and sets in the west.

HOW DOES IT WORK?

Magnets react with each other. Just think of how hard it is to pull them apart sometimes! Your magnetized needle starts to react to an enormous magnetic field—the one around the Earth. Your magnetic compass lines up along the north-south line of the Earth's magnetic field. As you saw when you marked your disc, once you find north, you can find the other three directions.

WHAT HAPPENS IF...?

Eventually, your magnetized needle will lose its magnetic force. You can try different ways of making it last longer, though. Predict whether rubbing the needle for longer will have an effect. What about using a stronger magnet?

REAL-LIFE SCIENCE

If you're lucky, you can see the Earth's magnetic field in action. Northern and Southern Lights are like dramatic firework displays in the night sky. These displays occur when charged particles from the Sun reach the Earth's magnetic field. Some of them rush through the atmosphere near the magnetic poles. They react with gases to produce bright lights.

Electric UFO

For years, engineers have tried to design aircrafts that fly silently and don't send nasty gases into the atmosphere. This experiment might set you on the path to finding the secret—you might even have a future in building flying saucers!

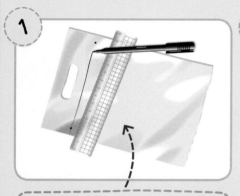

1 Lay the bag on a flat surface. Mark a dot on each long edge of the bag about three finger-widths down from one of the open corners.

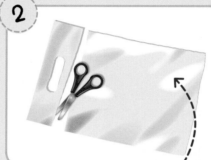

2 Carefully cut across the bag from dot to dot.

3 Blow up the balloon, tie it shut, then rub it against the wool quickly for about 15 seconds.

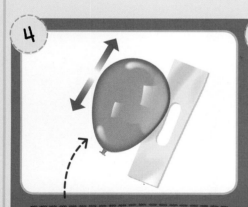

4 Lay the narrow plastic strip you just cut on the surface and rub it briskly with the balloon for 15 seconds.

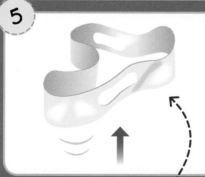

5 Holding the balloon in one hand, gently shake the strip so that it opens into a loop.

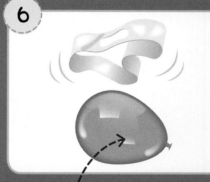

6 Toss the plastic loop into the air and quickly move the balloon under it. The balloon will keep it floating!

HOW DOES IT WORK?

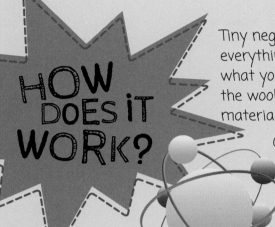

Tiny negatively charged electrons surround the atoms of everything around us, but they can be rubbed off easily. That's what you did when you rubbed the plastic and balloon with the wool. The wool lost some of its electrons but the other materials picked them up, which gave them a negative charge.

Objects with similar charges repel each other, which is what the balloon and plastic were doing. The plastic was pulled downwards by the force of gravity, but pushed back up by the action of the electrons.

REAL-LIFE SCIENCE

People have been reporting Unidentified Flying Objects (UFOs) for many years. Some people think these mysterious silent aircraft come from other planets. Do they exist? And if so, how can they travel across the sky and hover above us so silently? Maybe you have some thoughts on the subject now.

TOP TIPS!

You could try snipping your plastic strip so it has tassels. An object with many edges holds more charge.

WHAT HAPPENS IF...?

If this experiment is all about two objects rubbing together to get the same charge, what would happen if you only rubbed one of them — say, the balloon — but not the other? Make a prediction and test it yourself. How did it work?

The Magic Straws

You can harness the force of static electricity to perform some impressive tricks! See how you can command a straw to **rotate** by following this experiment.

YOU WILL NEED

- 2 straight plastic drinking straws
- Plastic drink bottle with screw-on cap
- Water
- Wool sweater or scarf

1

Fill the bottle halfway with water to make it more secure, then screw the cap on.

2

Quickly rub the plastic straws on the wool for about 1 minute.

3

Balance one straw on the lid of the bottle.

4

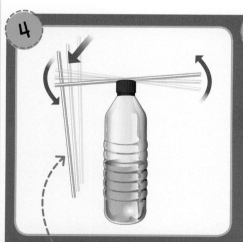

Hold the other straw and move it close to one end of the first straw, about 2 inches (5 cm) from it.

5

Move the second straw a little closer and watch the first one start to rotate. Keep the second straw about the same distance behind it. Try lifting the second straw and holding it on the other side of the resting straw. It should start to rotate the other way!

HOW DOES IT WORK?

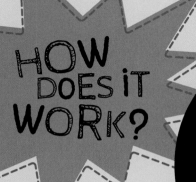

You've probably got a good idea about how static electricity works by now. Rubbing something like a balloon or a straw against wool causes electrons to jump from the wool. In this case, both straws gained a lot of electrons, which have a negative charge. When you lowered one electron-packed straw close to another, they pushed each other away. And you got one to chase the other around and around!

WHAT HAPPENS IF...?

Instead of lowering a second straw towards the first one, use your index finger. The straw will be attracted to your finger instead of repelled! Why? Because your finger has enough positively charged protons to attract the negatively charged electrons on the straw.

REAL-LIFE SCIENCE

The whole process of "opposites attracting" and "likes repelling" lies at the heart of many industries and engineering projects. It can even help keep the skies a little cleaner. Power plants have highly positively charged wires stretched across their chimneys. Tiny bits of ash and waste float past, picking up a positive charge. Just ahead lie negatively charged collection plates, which attract the ash and dirt and keep it from escaping into the outer air.

Electro-Music

Have you ever heard grown-ups complaining that pop music is "all electric"? Well, here's a chance to "generate" some electric music of your own! If anyone complains, you can say you're just demonstrating science.

YOU WILL NEED

- Cooking foil
- Balloon
- Mixing bowl (about 10 inches/25 cm in diameter)
- Elastic band, big enough to stretch around the bowl

1

Tear off a strip of foil large enough to cover the top of the bowl with a little extra foil over the sides. Rest it on the top of the bowl.

2

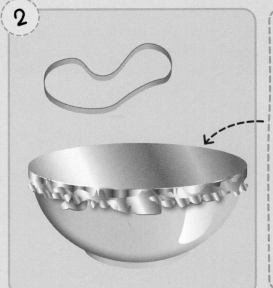

Wrap the extra bits over the edge of the bowl and secure it with the elastic band. Make the bit across the top of the bowl as tight as possible, like a drum. Tear off a much smaller strip of foil and then tear it further into pieces about the size of your thumbnail. Collect five or six of these small bits of foil.

3

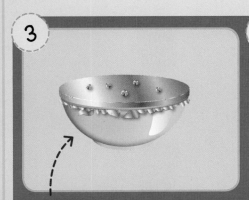

Scrunch those small bits of foil into loose balls the size of small peas. Don't squeeze them too tightly, then lay them on the foil surface covering the bowl.

4

Blow up the balloon, tie it shut, and rub it against your hair for 30 seconds.

5

Lower and raise the balloon (with the rubbed side facing down) up and down over the bowl. Watch and listen as the foil balls jump up and fall back down on the "drum" you've made!

26

HOW DOES IT WORK?

This demonstration of static electricity introduces a new feature—sound. The electric power source for the experiment was your hair! Rubbing it caused lots of electrons to attach to the balloon. That gave the "rubbed" side of the balloon a negative charge from the electrons. The protons of the metal foil were drawn to the negatively charged balloon—but only the loose bits of foil could actually jump up to it. That's because you'd attached the base to the bowl with the elastic band. And when the balls hit the flat foil, they produce vibrations in the air—which we hear as sound.

WHAT HAPPENS IF...?

Here are two variations of the experiment. Predict what will happen and then try them out!

1. Use the same type of balloon, but don't rub it against your hair.

2. Make tightly-wound foil balls that are about four times as large as the first balls.

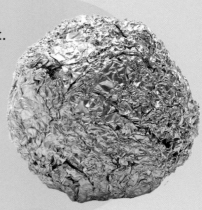

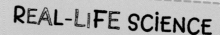

REAL-LIFE SCIENCE

This experiment has produced a very basic electric drum. Since the 1960s, musicians and engineers have teamed up to produce advanced electric drums. The drummer hits pads that just look like rubber, but inside are magnets that convert the "hits" into electrical signals. Those signals are sent along wires to speakers that turn them back into sounds.

A Switch in Time

If you're trying to be environmentally friendly and save energy, you'll know to turn off all the unused lights in the house. Here's a chance to see what happens when you flip those switches on and off!

1

Lay the paper clip on the card. Use a pencil to mark each end, just inside the paper clip loops.

2

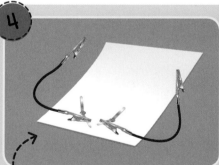

Use the pencil to poke a hole through each mark.

3

Push a paper fastener through each hole and then open up the wings of each fastener. This card/fastener combination will be your switch.

4

Connect one alligator clip to one wing of each fastener.

5

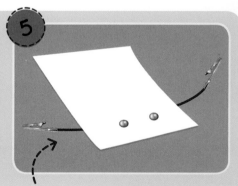

Lay the switch down on a table with the unfolded wings facing down.

28

6

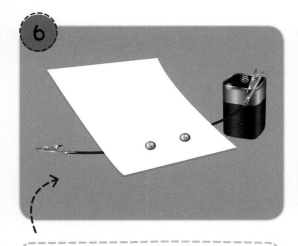

Attach the other end of one of those two clips to a battery terminal.

7

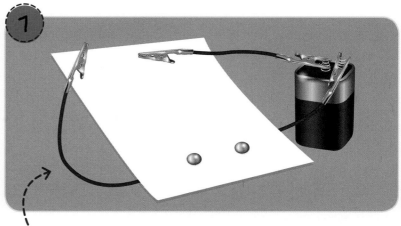

Attach one end of the third alligator clip (which hasn't been clipped to the switch) to the other battery terminal.

8

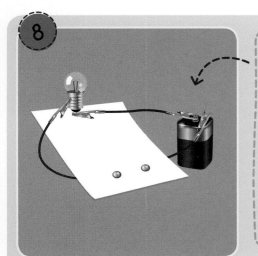

Have one friend hold the bulb. Touch one of the clips to the base of the bulb and the other to the metal side of the bulb. The light will not be on at this point.

9

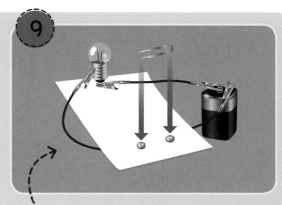

Have your second friend place the paper clip on the switch, so that it touches both metal fasteners.

10

The switch has turned the light on!

The voltage of this experiment is very low, but you can wear the rubber gloves as an extra safety precaution to prevent any shock.

Continued

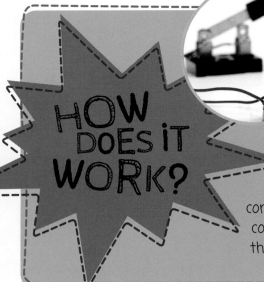

HOW DOES IT WORK?

You just created an electrical circuit! What's more, you showed what happens when that circuit is broken. Remember that electrons can flow from one object to another, provided that those objects can conduct the electrons. A circuit is just such a pathway, with electrons traveling along wires and through metal objects. The energy can power objects, such as the bulb. The paper clip conducts electricity, so the bulb lights up when the paper clip completes the circuit by linking both metal fasteners on the card. And it switches the bulb off when it's removed!

TOP TIP!

You can buy a bulb holder from a hardware store so you don't have to touch the clips to the bulb by hand.

REAL-LIFE SCIENCE

Every time you walk into a room and turn on the lights, you're using an electrical switch. In fact, you'll normally hear those devices described as switches even by people who don't understand electric circuits. This experiment operated on safe, low voltages but switches can become life-savers when they are used to cut off power in high-voltage equipment.

WHAT HAPPENS IF...?

If you had enough bulbs, alligator clips, and helpers, you could add more bulbs to your circuit. Will all the bulbs shine as brightly? Make predictions and record your results.

Glossary

acid A substance that has particular properties, such as being able to dissolve some metals.

artificial A human-made object.

atom The smallest particle that can exist.

battery A container that provides electricity.

circuit The closed path that an electrical current follows.

conductor A material that can transmit heat or electricity.

electron A negatively charged particle that forms part of an atom.

force The strength of a particular energy at work.

friction The force that causes a moving object to slow down.

gas A substance that can expand to fill any shape.

gravity The force that causes all objects to be attracted to each other.

hypothesis An explanation for an observation that can be tested.

particle A very tiny piece of matter.

predict To say what will happen in the future or as a result of an action.

propeller A device made up of a shaft and two or more angled blades that, when turned, moves a boat or aircraft.

rotate To turn or spin around a central point.

static electricity Electricity that is held or discharged (sent off) by an object.

zinc A chemical element that is a silvery white metal.

Further Information

Books to read

Electricity by Steve Parker (DK Children, 2013)

Horrible Science: Shocking Electricity by Nick Arnold (Scholastic, 2014)

Mind Webs: Electricity and Magnetism by Anna Claybourne (Wayland, 2016)

Websites

https://www.education.com/science-fair/electricity-and-magnetism/
Find more incredible experiments with electricity and magnets at this awesome site!

http://www.physics4kids.com/index.html
Learn about fascinating scientific principles, including electricity and magnetism!

Publisher's note to educators and parents: Our editors have carefully reviewed these websites to ensure that they are suitable for students. Many websites change frequently, however, and we cannot guarantee that a site's future contents will continue to meet our high standards of quality and educational value. Be advised that students should be closely supervised whenever they access the Internet.

Index

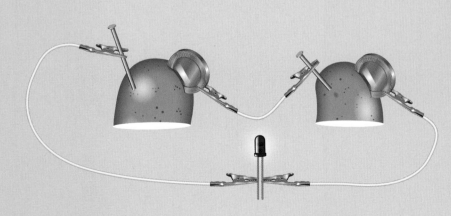